GOALKEEPERS

JONNY ZUCKER

FULL FLIGHT

Badger Publishing Limited
Oldmedow Road,
Hardwick Industrial Estate,
King's Lynn PE30 4JJ
Telephone: 01438 791037

www.badgerlearning.co.uk

2 4 6 8 10 9 7 5 3 1

Goalkeepers ISBN 978-1-85880-928-1 (second edition) 2013

Text © Jonny Zucker 2002
Complete work © Badger Publishing Limited 2002

Publisher: Susan Ross
Senior Editor: Danny Pearson
Designer: Fiona Grant

Photos: Cover image: East News / Rex Features
Page 4: Darko Vojinovic/AP/Press Association Images
Page 7: Bernat Armangue/AP/Press Association Images
Page 8: Stefan Rousseau/PA Archive/Press Association Images
Page 10: Revierfoto/DPA/Press Association Images
Page 11: Peter Dejong/AP/Press Association Images
Page 13: Phil Noble/PA Archive/Press Association Images
Page 14: VIRGINIE LEFOUR/Belga/Press Association Images
Page 15: Neal Simpson/EMPICS Sport
Page 17: Laurence Griffiths/EMPICS Sport
Page 19: S&G/S&G and Barratts/EMPICS Sport
Page 21: Neal Simpson/EMPICS Sport
Page 23: Matthias Schrader/AP/Press Association Images
Page 24: Antonio Calanni/AP/Press Association Images
Page 25: Ivan Sekretarev/AP/Press Association Images
Page 26: Neal Simpson/EMPICS Sport
Page 29: EMPICS SPORTS PHOTOS/EMPICS Sport
Page 30: Martin Meissner/AP/Press Association Images

Attempts to contact all copyright holders have been made.
If any omitted would care to contact Badger Learning, we will be
happy to make appropriate arrangements.

GOALKEEPERS

JONNY ZUCKER

Contents

Badger
L E A R N I N G

I. THE GOALKEEPER'S KIT

To be a goalkeeper you need some basic football kit.

Boots for grass and trainers for a hard surface are needed. Shin pads are very important as they can stop a goalkeeper getting badly hurt.

Tracksuit bottoms are useful because they protect your legs better than shorts. This is very true in a playground!

A goalkeeper's top with elbow pads can make your life as a goalkeeper a little bit safer. Goalkeeping gloves are important because they protect your hands and hold the ball well.

2. GOALKEEPING RULES

The back-pass rule is one of the most important for goalies. If one of your own players passes back to you and you handle the ball, the other side get a direct free kick. This happens, even if you touched the ball very near to your goal.

If one of your players heads the ball back to you, it is OK to use your hands.

If you trip a player in your penalty area, and you are the last player on your team, this means a lot of trouble!

Not only do the other team get a penalty, but the referee will probably send you off as well.

Muteba Kidiaba is shown the red card

3. THE GREATEST SAVE?

Many people say that the save by the England goalkeeper Gordon Banks from Brazil's Pelé is the best save of all time.

Gordon Banks and Pelé holding a photo of the famous save

It happened in a match of the 1970 World Cup finals.

As the ball was crossed over to Pelé from the right, he jumped very high, and headed the ball down at great speed towards the England goal.

It looked as if Banks had no chance because he was diving the wrong way. But somehow he was able to change direction, stretch his body and flick the ball away.

4. 'HANDLING' THE BALL

Goalkeepers are the only players who can touch the ball with their hands when it is 'in play'.

If the ball is inside their penalty area they can use their hands. If it is outside their penalty area and they touch the ball with their hands, then this gives away a 'direct' free kick.

In the early days of football, all of the players on the pitch could use their hands. In 1863 all players could touch the ball, and a free kick was given if one team 'touched the ball down' over the other team's goal line – like a 'try' in rugby.

5. THE KING OF THE PENALTY AREA

Some goalkeepers are not very loud.
They have a quiet word with their
defenders from time to time and tell
them where they should make a wall
at free kicks.

Other goalkeepers are very noisy.
The most famous king of the penalty
area is Peter Schmeichel. When he played
for Manchester United, he shouted and
screamed at his defenders to do what
he wanted.

When one of his defenders made a
mistake and Schmeichel let a goal in,
he would make it very clear who was
to blame.

Peter Schmeichel celebrates with his teammates after
winning the Champions League final in 1999

Sometimes his defenders took all of this yelling, but at other times they shouted back at him!

6. THE NUMBER ONE SHIRT

Goalkeepers wear the number one shirt because they are the first player as the team stands on the pitch. Reserve goalkeepers wear different numbers.

Many number one shirts are one colour, and are sometimes the same colour as the rest of the team's shirts.

One ex-goalkeeper famous for his colourful shirts is David Seaman who played for Arsenal and England. He has worn a number one shirt that was a mix of very bright colours.

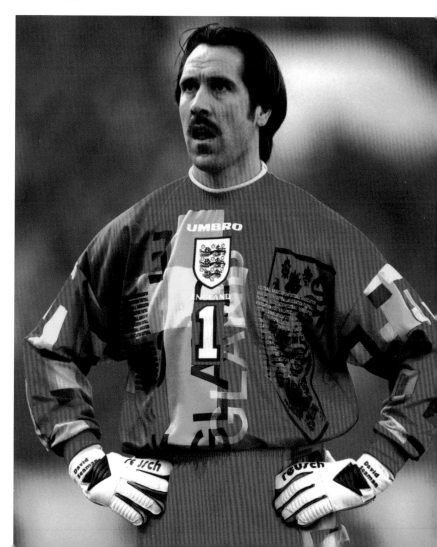

7. GOALKEEPERS AS GOALSCORERS

There have been times when goalkeepers have scored goals.

In the 1970s Pat Jennings, who was then playing for Tottenham, took a very big goal kick which flew right to the other end of the ground and over the other goalkeeper's head.

Peter Schmeichel, when he played for Manchester United, liked to go up the field for free kicks when his team badly needed a goal.

In one game, he helped his team in this way. When a free kick was lobbed into the penalty area, Schmeichel was there waiting. He jumped up and headed the ball in.

8. THE CAT

Some goalkeepers have nicknames.

The most famous goalkeeping nickname was the one given to the Chelsea goalkeeper Peter Bonetti in the 1960s and 1970s.

Bonetti was called 'The Cat' because of the way he could spring around his penalty area. Like a cat, he could jump very high and dive very far, and because of this great skill, he was able to make some amazing saves.

It wasn't just the Chelsea fans and players who called him this name.

Wherever he went in the world, football fans would watch him play and talk about 'The Cat'.

Peter 'The Cat' Bonetti'

9. THE PENALTY SAVE

Many goalkeepers say the thing they like best is to save a penalty.

In the 1988 FA Cup final, Liverpool were given a penalty. The ball was kicked very hard, but the Wimbledon goalkeeper Dave Beasant was very fast off his line. He dived to his left and saved the penalty.

He was the first goalkeeper to save a penalty in an FA Cup final. His Wimbledon team went on to win the cup.

The 1994 World Cup, held in the USA, saw the first World Cup final to be decided on penalties.

Brazil beat Italy after Roberto Baggio hit his penalty over the crossbar.

Roberto Baggio said after the game:
"I was so tired that I tried to hit the ball too hard."

10. GOALIE PRACTICE

Here are some good tips to improve your goalkeeping skills.

1. Get a friend to take shots against you along the ground. As the ball comes towards you, kneel down on one leg and lean over the ball. When the ball gets to you, collect it in both hands and hug it to your body.

2. Have someone take high corners towards the goal. As the ball flies in, jump up and catch the ball. As soon as it's in your hands, bring the ball down into your body.

3. Ask another player to take higher shots against you, and practise tipping the ball over the crossbar with one or both hands. For shots that go to your left or right, try to tip the ball round one of the goal posts.

Have ten high balls kicked in towards your goal from the left or the right. Punch the first five with one hand, and the second five with both hands. Punch the ball as far away as you can.

5. It is very important to practise your kicking skills. Take ten kicks with the ball on the ground, and then ten kicks from your hands. Also practise your throwing. Try ten underarm throws and then ten throws from your shoulder.

II. CLEAN SHEETS AND NOT-SO-CLEAN SHEETS

A 'clean sheet' means a game where a goalkeeper has not let in any goals. It is a goalkeeper's number one aim to keep a clean sheet in a football match.

In Spain, in 1991, Abel Resino, the Atlético Madrid goalkeeper, went for 1,275 minutes without letting in a goal. That's 14 clean sheets in a row!

In a Scottish cup match in 1885, the Bon Accord team's goalkeeper did not keep a clean sheet. In fact, he let in 36 goals! The final score was Arbroath 36, Bon Accord nil.

12. A SPECIAL SAVE

Some goalkeepers create their own special saves. One of the most famous is that dreamed up by the Colombian keeper René Higuita in the 1990s.

To do this move, he waited until a high ball was kicked in towards his goal. He watched the ball very carefully for a few seconds.

He then allowed the ball to go over his head. When the ball was just behind him, he dived forward, bringing his legs up behind his head and smashing the ball away with them.

Because this move reminded him of the body shape of a deadly creature, he called this save 'The Scorpion'.

René Higuita doing 'The Scorpion'

13. THE TEN BEST GOALKEEPERS OF ALL TIME

Everyone has a different idea about who are the ten best goalkeepers of all time. Some people say the goalkeepers of long ago were braver and more skilful.

Iker Casillas lifting the World Cup

Other people say that the goalkeepers of today are fitter and better athletes.

Here is one list of the possible ten best keepers of all time:

1. Iker Casillas – Spain
2. Gianluigi Buffon – Italy
3. Peter Shilton – England
4. Peter Schmeichel – Denmark
5. Fabien Barthez – France
6. Lev Yashin – Russia
7. Petr Cech – Czech Republic
8. Dino Zoff – Italy
9. Gordon Banks – England
10. Edwin van der Sar – Netherlands

INDEX